October 1986

For Randy,

I found this book at Westminster Abbey and felt it was a gift to me... in its breadth of expression to you... what a treasure our friendship is.

With gratefulness and
deep affection,
Janet

THE GIFT OF FRIENDS

Written and compiled by Marion Stroud

A LION BOOK

Copyright © 1983 Lion Publishing

Published by
Lion Publishing plc
Icknield Way, Tring, Herts, England
ISBN 0 85648 543 8
Albatross Books Pty Ltd
PO Box 320, Sutherland, NSW 2232, Australia
ISBN 0 86760 436 0

First edition 1983
Reprinted 1985, 1986

Acknowledgements
The photographs in this book are reproduced by permission of the following
photographers and organizations:
Art Directors Photo Library: Title page, 'Who needs friends?', 'His, hers and ours'
and cover photograph.
British Tourist Authority: 'Built to last', 'Take time'.
Sonia Halliday Photographs/Sonia Halliday: 'Celebration of friendship'.
Image Bank: 'Reunion'.
Lion Publishing/David Alexander: 'Words' (left-hand page), 'The stoning', 'Be still'.
Jean-Luc Ray: 'Words' (right-hand page, above and below), 'The best part',
'On the outside', 'Handle with care'.
John and Patricia Woolverton: 'Benediction'.
ZEFA: 'Friendship is an art', 'Someone special', 'Just the way I am', 'Listening',
'An understanding heart', 'Honesty'.
All remaining photographs by Lion Publishing/Jon Willcocks.

Bible quotations as follows: Luke 10:30,33-34 ('Who needs friends?') from *Holy
Bible, New International Version*, copyright 1978 New York International Bible
Society; John 15:13, Isaiah 53:4-6 and Romans 5:8-11 ('God's friends'), 1 John
3:16,18 ('Love in action') and Proverbs 17:17 ('Handle with care') from *Good News
Bible*, copyright 1966, 1971 and 1976 American Bible Society, published by Bible
Societies/Collins.

Other copyright material as follows: 'Leave it all quietly to God' from Ruth Bell
Graham, *Sitting By My Laughing Fire*, copyright ©1977 by Ruth Bell Graham, used
by permission of Word Books, Publisher, Waco, Texas; 'The stoning' from *Hold Me
Up a Little Longer, Lord* by Marjorie Holmes, copyright ©1977 by Marjorie Holmes
Mighell, reprinted by permission of Doubleday & Company, Inc., and Hodder and
Stoughton Ltd (*Lord, Let Me Love*); 'Circle of light' from 'Minimaxims for My
Godson' in *A Touch of Wonder* by Arthur Gordon, copyright ©1974 by Fleming H.
Revell Company, originally in Readers' Digest, copyright ©1969 by Readers' Digest
Association; 'Healing for loneliness' from *Alone—A Search for Joy* by Katie F. Wiebe,
Lakeland Paperbacks.

Every effort has been made to trace and contact copyright owners. If there are any
inadvertent omissions in the acknowledgements, we apologize to those concerned.

Printed and bound in Italy

A faithful friend is the medicine of life.

The Book of Ecclesiasticus

CELEBRATION OF FRIENDSHIP

No medicine is more valuable, none more efficacious,
none better suited to the cure of all our temporal ills
than a friend, to whom we may turn for consolation in
time of trouble, and with whom we may share our
happiness in times of joy.

Ailred of Rievaulx

A man with few friends is only half developed; there are whole sides of his nature which are locked up and have never been expressed. He cannot unlock them himself; he cannot even discover them; friends alone can stimulate him and open him.

Randolph Bourne

Since there is nothing so well worth having as friends, never lose a chance to make them. For men are brought into constant contact with one another, and friends help and foes hinder at times and places where you least expect it.

Francesco Guicciardini

FRIENDSHIP IS AN ART

I wish I had a magic formula for making friendship happen. I don't . . .

Friendship is not something about which we can learn rules. Friendship and loving are arts, but not some kind of commercial art so we can impress people. Friends are free individuals who risk being themselves with each other— people who share their uniqueness and delight in seeing each other grow as a result of their shared relationship . . .

Without friends, we cannot be fully human. We have to be, and to have, friends.

David Sammons

BUILT TO LAST

'Deep friendships are rare today. We have acquaintances and casual friends, but few of us enjoy intimate life-changing relationships that last.'

No real and lasting friendship just happens; it is built. And the quality of the bricks we use will decide the quality of the friendship.

The first essential quality of a lasting friendship is giving. My friend is not just someone who meets my need, but the one whose needs I can meet. True friendship begins with the decision to *be* a friend, not to have a friend.

A second quality of lasting friendship is the breadth of interests that we share. If we are real friends, we will allow no jealousy or competition to warp or twist our relationship but will work together, sharing a commitment to a common cause.

The third vital quality is encouragement. I need to be right there with my friend when life is hard, giving help and support, but also encouraging him to look away from the difficult circumstances to an all-sufficient God. If I fail him at this point, I fail him in his deepest need.

Dostoevsky wrote, 'To love a person means to see him as God intended him to be.' And this is the test of true friendship. Not just to see my friend like that, but to act in such a way that, because we are friends, he will be more able to translate the potential into reality.

SOMEONE SPECIAL

How good of God that he should choose to give you to me as my friend. That out of all the people in the world, he should have caused our paths to cross, our circumstances to intertwine, our minds to spark against each other—so that when we talk, there are so often fresh ways of thinking, new insights into love and life, and faith.

Thank you for simply being there, on the dark days—and in the sunshine: available, ready to listen, to laugh, to weep with me, to pray.

Thank you for an arm flung round my shoulders, a funny card, a bunch of flowers, a cake. Knowing when to sympathize and when to haul me back to my feet, and give me a push in the right direction.

Thank you for sharing your joys, problems, pleasure and pain with me. For letting me know that I am important to you, that my contribution counts.

You are someone special. Because of our friendship I have grown as a person. I hope that you have too.

Thank you for being my friend.

TAKE TIME

Friendship requires communication between friends. Otherwise it can neither be born nor exist.

Francis de Sales

There is a definite process by which one made people into friends and it involved talking to them and listening to them for hours at a time.

Rebecca West

It is the steady and merciless increase of occupations, the augmented speed at which we are always trying to live, the crowding of each day with more work than it can profitably hold which has cost us, among other things, the undisturbed enjoyment of friends. Friendship takes time and we have no time to give it.

Agnes Repplier

JUST THE WAY I AM

Friendship with oneself is all-important because without it one cannot be friends with anyone else in the world.

Eleanor Roosevelt

Be gentle, patient, humble and courteous to all, but especially be gentle and patient with yourself. I think that many of your troubles arise from an exaggerated anxiety, a secret impatience with your own faults; and this restlessness, when once it has got possession of your mind, is the cause of numberless trifling faults, which worry you, and go on adding to your burden until it becomes unbearable. I would have you honest in checking and correcting yourself, but at the same time patient under the consciousness of your frailty.

Père Hyacinthe Besson

God loves and forgives me and accepts me, just the way I am, unconditionally. And he will love me into perfection.

Because he loves and forgives and accepts me as I am, then I love (in the right way) and accept myself just the way I am . . . in the body he has given me, with my limitations and imperfections—because he can use them as a showcase for his grace and glory.

Elisabeth Strachen

PEACE

Leave it all quietly to God...
the past mistakes
that left
the scars.
All bitterness
beyond control,
that mars
His peace,
demands its toll.
Confessed to Him
...and left...
it would,
like all things
work together
for my good,
and bring release.
I would be whole.
So
Leave it all quietly to God...

Ruth Bell Graham

LISTENING

It is impossible to over-emphasise the immense need men have to be really listened to, to be taken seriously, to be understood. . . No one can develop freely in this world and find a full life, without feeling understood by at least one person.

Paul Tournier

Listen with love—if you find the one who speaks irritating, tiresome or unlovable, your attitude will colour what you hear.

Listen with your eyes as well as with your ears—only a small proportion of our meaning is expressed in the words we choose. The way we stand or sit, smile or scowl, clench our fists or twist our legs into knots also speaks volumes.

Listening is hard work—never discuss a problem standing up, or on an empty stomach! Choose the right time and place, and give your friend your full attention—even if you have heard it all before.

Listen with understanding—we all want to know that we have been heard, that our feelings, anxieties and hurts have been shared. If you don't grasp what your friend is saying clearly, ask questions until you do.

Listen often; listen without lecturing or advising; listen with all you have. Remember: to listen in such a way that the other person can be totally open, and feel absolutely free to share his deepest needs, is one of the greatest services that one human being can do for another.

God gave us two ears but only one mouth. . .[perhaps] a divine indication that we should listen twice as much as we talk.

John Powell

WORDS

Speech is God's gift.
We shall have to account for it.
It is through words
that we communicate with each other
and we reveal what we are.
We haven't the right to be silent,
but speaking is a serious matter
and we must weigh our words
in the sight of God.

Michel Quoist

THE STONING

Lord, I detest myself right now.

For I've just come from a luncheon where four of us spent most of our time criticizing a mutual friend. Her faults, her eccentricities, how extravagant and undependable she is. How she spoils her children, how vain and eager she always is to be attractive to men.

And though a lot of these things are true (Lord, they really are) I found myself wondering even as I joined in: Who are we to judge? Isn't every one of us guilty of at least some of the very same things? Was that why we attacked her with such relish? (Dear Lord, I'm so ashamed.) Because it made us feel a little bit better ourselves to brandish the defects of somebody so much 'worse'.

Well, I don't feel better about myself now. I keep thinking of what Jesus said to the men about to stone the adulterous woman: 'Which of you is without sin?' Yet there we sat, self-righteous, stoning our sister with words.

How, Lord, can I make amends?

I long to call her up and beg her forgiveness, but that would be a terrible mistake. She would be so hurt, so much damage would be done. No, all I can do is to ask *your* forgiveness. And pray for her.

Help her, strengthen her, bless her. Don't let her ever know what we said about her, please.

And oh, Lord, put more compassion in my heart, guard my tongue. Don't let me ever again join in stoning a sister—or anyone—with words.

Marjorie Holmes

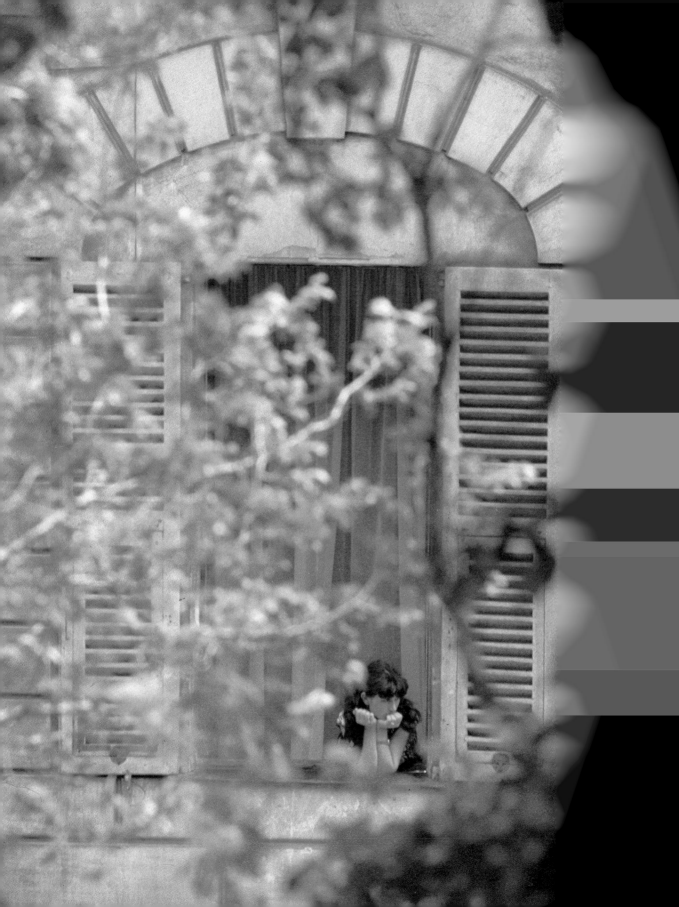

AN UNDERSTANDING HEART

How rarely we weigh our neighbour in the same balance in which we weigh ourselves.

Thomas à Kempis

Who seeks a faultless friend remains friendless.

Turkish proverb

To find a friend one must close one eye.
To keep him—two!

Norman Douglas

Do not judge others, or you too will be judged.

Jesus: from the New Testament

It should be part of our private ritual to devote a quarter hour every day to the enumeration of the good qualities of our friends. When we are not *active* we fall back idly upon defects, even of those whom we most love.

Mark Rutherford

Grant that I may have an understanding heart and be able to show compassion to those whose sins may not be the same as mine. Keep me ever mindful of the faults in my own life, lest I devote my attention to condemning others.

Brian Hession

CIRCLE OF LIGHT

One Sunday morning, drowsing in the back pew of a little country church, I dimly heard the old preacher urge his flock to 'stop worrying about your own halo and shine up your neighbour's!' And it left me sitting up, wide-awake, because it struck me as just about the best eleven-word formula for getting along with people that I ever heard.

I like it for its implication that everyone, in some area of life, has a halo that's worth watching for and acknowledging. I like it for the picture it conjures up: everybody industriously polishing away at everybody else's little circle of divine light. I like it for the firm way it shifts the emphasis from self to interest and concern for others. Finally, I like it because it reflects a deep truth: people have a tendency to become what you expect them to be.

Arthur Gordon

THE BEST PART

You give but little when you give of your possessions. It is when you give of yourself that you truly give.

It seems to me that the one privilege of friendship is . . . to make the best of friends, to encourage and believe in them, to hand on the pleasant things.

A.C. Benson

'We must be purposely kind and generous, or we miss the best part of existence. The heart that goes out of itself gets large and full of joy. This is the great secret of the inner life. We do ourselves the most good doing something for others.'

HEALING FOR LONELINESS

Loneliness is the common enemy of all humankind...it is a universal feeling. It occurs among the great and the lowly, the rich and the poor, and even among the married...every heart at times feels the ache of loneliness. Even Jesus was lonely and longed for the disciples to stay awake and watch with him before the betrayal and crucifixion.

The real cure for loneliness is the healing interaction of two personalities. Loneliness leaves when there is sharing of deeper needs, struggles and joy. Friends can bring you courage and hope that is more necessary to life than happiness. 'To live is to love', so don't hole up in your house or apartment. Join clubs, organizations and activities to the extent that you can enjoy and accommodate these in your schedule. Force yourself to move out of your home at least once a day.

Visit the old, the sick, the elderly. Take your neighbour a new dish. Begin a regular correspondence...remember that what you do *for* someone helps that person. What you do *with* them helps you both. Take time to make friends with individuals who might ordinarily be outside of your social group. The Good Samaritan has lived in memory for centuries without a name. The best friends are not always the most important people.

See yourself as a person worthy of love, even if no one at the moment seems to be tripping over his feet with a rose in his teeth to tell you so. But recognize that loneliness won't disappear overnight. It may have to be swept out...each day.

There may be times when you will take a few minutes to weep...but only a few minutes. Then get on with living again. And in living hang on to Christ as Lord and Saviour. He...above all others...can be your personal friend.

Katie F. Wiebe

WHO NEEDS FRIENDS?

Jesus said: 'A man was going down from Jerusalem to Jericho, when he fell into the hands of robbers. They stripped him...beat him and went away, leaving him half-dead...A Samaritan... came where the man was; and...took pity on him. He went to him and bandaged his wounds, pouring on oil and wine. Then he put the man on his own donkey, brought him to an inn and took care of him.'
Luke's Gospel

Lord God,
Please show your love to that man we met today. You remember him. The one who looked so lonely and yet insisted that he had no need of any friends. His words keep echoing through my mind.

'Friends?' he said. 'Who needs them? There's no such thing as friendship. Just people, out for what they can get. Interested in you while you've got something to give them and then...nothing. Don't talk to me about friends. I keep myself to myself. That way I may not do much laughing, but I don't cry any more.'

What happened to him in the past, Lord, to make him react in this way? What are the hurts that keep him (and many like him) locked up inside themselves, afraid of others, afraid of love, afraid of life itself?

Only you can deal with the past, Lord.
Only you can pour in the oil and wine that will heal the wounds.
And so we can leave him to you...or can we?
How can your arms reach out to him...unless it is through our arms?
How can your hands touch him...unless it is through us?
How can your love be demonstrated...except through people?
Perhaps he will only understand your care when he sees ours.

Lord God, please show your love to that man we met today—through us.

CHANGING THE WORLD

Grant, O Lord, that none may love Thee less this day because of me.
That never word or act of mine may turn one soul from Thee.
And ever daring, yet one other grace would I implore.
That many souls this day, because of me, may love Thee more.

Medieval prayer

I am only one, but still I am one. I cannot do
everything, but still I can do something, and
because I cannot do everything, let me not
refuse to do the something that I can do.

Edward Everett Hale

As one person I cannot change the world. But
I can change the world for one person.

GOD'S FRIENDS

The greatest love a person can have for his
friends is to give his life for them.

Jesus: from the New Testament

But he [Jesus] endured the suffering
    that should have been ours,
    the pain that we should have borne.
All the while we thought that his suffering
    was punishment sent by God.
But because of our sins he was wounded,
    beaten because of the evil we did.
We are healed by the punishment he suffered,
    made whole by the blows he received.
All of us were like sheep that were lost,
    each of us going his own way.
But the Lord made the punishment fall on him,
    the punishment all of us deserved.

The Book of Isaiah

God has shown us how much he loves us...We
were God's enemies, but he made us his friends
through the death of his Son. Now that we are
God's friends...we rejoice because of what
God has done through our Lord Jesus Christ.

Paul: from the New Testament

THE PERFECT FRIEND

Lord God, you are the perfect Friend,
Other friends may misunderstand or let me down,
But you never disappoint me.
When I am in need of help or encouragement,
You always have the right words for the situation.
You understand me completely,
There isn't a thought in my mind
*   or an intention of my heart*
*   that you are not aware of.*
I am never alone
*   because you are always there beside me.*
Neither day nor night,
*   distance nor circumstances can ever separate us.*
In your total knowledge
*   you can lead me in a path of absolute safety,*
*   and so I can follow you with complete confidence.*
When you point out my faults you do it with love.
That love to me is like the sunshine
*   that lights up the world on a spring morning,*
*   dispelling the gloom of winter.*
You bring joy into my life.
You are my friend;
I give you thanks and praise you, Lord.

BE STILL

Time for myself...Why is it that I find it so hard to take time for myself? Time to *be*, rather than to *do*. Time to think, to talk to God, and most of all to be silent in his presence while he talks to me.

You know how it is, Lord! There is always so much to be fitted in. People to be seen...work to be done...obligations to fulfil! It is so difficult to distinguish between the urgent and the important. And often what is urgent elbows its way to the forefront of my day and the important gets trampled on in the rush.

Slow me down, Lord. Teach me the art of creating islands of stillness, in which I can absorb the beauty of everyday things: clouds, trees, a snatch of music. Prompt me to lift up my heart to you in a moment of thankfulness. Impress upon my mind that there is more to life than packing every moment with activity, and help me to fence in some part of my day with quietness. And please talk to me and help me to listen, so that I take your peace rather than my confusion back with me into the hurly-burly of a hurting world.

To go up alone into the mountain and come back as an ambassador to the world, has ever been the method of humanity's best friends.

Evelyn Underhill

'Go home to your friends,' [Jesus] told him, 'and tell them what wonderful things God has done for you; and how merciful he has been.'

Mark's Gospel

COMFORTABLE SILENCE

I always felt that the great high privilege, relief and comfort of friendship was that one had to explain nothing.

Katherine Mansfield

Oh, the comfort, the inexpressible comfort of feeling safe with a person, having neither to weigh thoughts nor measure words but pour them all right out just as they are, chaff and grain together, knowing that a faithful hand will take and sift them, keep what is worth keeping and then with the breath of kindness blow the rest away.

George Eliot

True friendship comes when silence between two people is comfortable.

Dave Tyson Gentry

To know someone here or there with whom you feel there is understanding in spite of distances or thoughts unexpressed—that can make of this earth a garden.

Johann Wolfgang von Goethe

REUNION

'Together!' What a beautiful word that is. Somehow it holds within it the joy, the comfort, the quiet security and the sheer fun and excitement that we have experienced this weekend.

You have blessed us with many friends, Lord. But out of a host of acquaintances and a smaller number of closer friends, there are these rare and special ones with whom our hearts feel joyfully and totally at home. Thank you that after all these years we have been able to spend time with two of them; and that neither time nor distance has touched the love, the understanding and the indescribable sense of belonging to each other that binds us together as your children.

Thank you that there was not strangeness at our meeting, no reserve; just a gentle slipping back into the comfortable closeness that is such a special thing about this particular relationship.

Thank you, Lord, for the laughter and the lively discussions—we don't have to agree on every point in order to keep our friendship intact! Thank you for the sharing and the caring that runs so deep. And thank you that at the end of the day we could join hands and pray, bringing our joys and anxieties to you, who have given us this precious gift of friendship.

HONESTY

'How are you?' you ask, and I give you the standard reply.

'Fine, thanks!' I say, because your tone and the keys in your hand suggest that you haven't time to stop and listen; you're being polite rather than concerned. And so I don't tell you that everything in my world is grey today; that I'm worried sick about Johnny; I've had sharp words with the mechanic who only half-mended the car, and that the threat of redundancy looms large in my life.

If I thought that you really cared...I'd be so glad to talk to someone. To know that at this moment another human being felt what I am feeling, and understood. But I need a certain something from you—a word, a look, a touch—to unlock my lips and to enable me to tell you how I really feel.

And yet...it could be that I misjudge you. Perhaps by my pretence, I have denied you the opportunity of giving me what you would be so ready to give...if you knew.

The moment has passed now, but next time I'll try to be more willing to trust you. And when *I* ask 'How are you?' I'll try to read your answer in your eyes, your movements and your voice, as well as in your words. I'll be prepared to listen and to share your sorrow or your joy; to let you know that there is someone right beside you, who cares and wants to answer to your need.

ON THE OUTSIDE

Why, oh why are little girls so cruel to one another? Ganging up, promising everlasting friendship and then falling out, so that there always seems to be one on the edge of any group who is excluded, who hasn't any friends?

This week it is my child who is on the outside, Lord. She weeps and I want to weep with her. 'I don't want to go to school tomorrow,' she said, 'because I won't have a partner for drama. Kate doesn't like me any more; I haven't any friends.'

Why, Lord, must teachers make such a thing of choosing partners? Especially in a class in which there's an odd number of children. Why don't they arrange the groupings for a change, instead of leaving the popular ones to pair up and the others to do the best they can? Have they forgotten how much it hurts—to be the last one to be chosen?

Thank you, Lord, that this loneliness, for my child, is just a temporary thing. That usually she is one of the giggling, chattering group who do things together, gets invited to parties or out for overnight stays. While she is on the outside, Lord, help her to learn from it. To be more sympathetic to those who are often the odd ones. To discover how to offer friendship as well as to receive it. And, most of all, to know your friendship as a warm, comforting, living reality—always available.

'HIS, HERS AND OURS'

You have asked us what we think about friends for a married couple—the 'his 'n hers' variety, as well as the 'ours' and the 'yours'.

'Why should we need them?' one of you asks. 'Shouldn't a husband and wife be friends enough for one another?'

'Why should I give them up?' demands the other. 'They're part of my life and important to me!'

Before the whole issue becomes a battleground, and friends become enemies, let me share with you some discoveries that we have made over the years.

The crux of the matter seems to be that men and women view this whole business of friendship differently. Look around you and you will see what we mean. Many men have a number of casual friends but often see little need for 'soul-mates' with whom they share their thoughts, hopes and fears. That is a quality they look for in a wife! Whereas women of every age commonly keep a few close friends with whom they exchange confidences and discuss things that, they feel, only another woman could understand. Neither viewpoint is better than the other—just different.

This difference in outlook need not be a problem to a married couple, as long as they give first priority to their own relationship. We have found that we can offer each other a very special quality of friendship which no one else can duplicate, but, like any other friendship, it needs to be enjoyed, guarded and cared for enthusiastically if it is to achieve its full potential.

Of course we need to allow one another space for other people. Every friendship has its own unique contribution to make; we have each been enriched by the other's friends and their input into our lives, both individually and together.

Last of all, we have learned to pray for the gift of friends we can share. If 'his' or 'hers' can become truly 'ours', so that mutual love and caring binds you together with others, it is something for which to be deeply thankful. Friendships of this kind are a high privilege, and every marriage is the better and stronger for them.

LOVE IN ACTION

When a friend is in trouble, don't annoy him by asking if there is anything you can do. Think of something appropriate and do it.

E.W. Howe

So many people called or wrote or telephoned that summer.

'Your father was a good man,' they said. 'Parting hurts, but you can remember him with pride. If there is anything we can do... anything at all... don't hesitate to ask!' But we just couldn't stop to think what needed doing... and so we smiled and thanked them, struggling numbly on.

And then you came, bringing with you few words, no promises of future help or flowery phrases, but love, in the shape of a tool-box and a tin of cakes.

'You must have plenty to do,' you said. 'I'll look at the car, and see if I can sort out that rattle that is bothering you. You need a reliable car at a time like this. And don't bother about the house. Mary will look in on a Friday. She enjoys cleaning, and it will be one thing that you don't have to think about... until you want to.'

And so it was, all through the long, hot weeks. Our home was cared for and our ancient car maintained, while we embarked on all the extra duties that sudden death brings in its wake, comforted; not by hearing words but by seeing love... for love in action is surely love made visible.

This is how we know what love is: Christ gave his life for us. We too, then, ought to give our lives for our brothers!... Our love should not be just words and talk; it must be true love, which shows itself in action.

John: from the New Testament

HANDLE WITH CARE

People are lonely because they build walls instead of bridges.

Friendship is an art, and very few persons are born with a natural gift for it.

Kathleen Norris

Why am I afraid to tell you who I am? If I tell you who I am, you may not like who I am, and that is all that I have.

John Powell

A friend is one who knows all about you and loves you just the same.

Friends always show their love. What are brothers for if not to share trouble?

The Book of Proverbs

'A friend is the one who comes in when the whole world has gone out.'

Even from the best of human friends I must not ask for more than he can give.

Alban Goodier

Friends are lost by calling often and by calling seldom.

Scottish proverb

Good friendships are fragile things and require as much care as any other fragile and precious thing.

Randolph Bourne

BENEDICTION

May the road rise up to meet you,
may the wind be always at your back,
may the sun shine warm upon your face,
and the rain fall soft upon your fields,
and until we meet again
may God hold you in the palm of His hand.

Irish blessing